THE CHICAGO BULLS

BY

MARK STEWART

Content Consultant
Matt Zeysing
Historian and Archivist
The Naismith Memorial Basketball Hall of Fame

NORWOOD HOUSE PRESS

CHICAGO, ILLINOIS

Norwood House Press
P.O. Box 316598
Chicago, Illinois 60631

For information regarding Norwood House Press, please visit our website at:
www.norwoodhousepress.com or call 866-565-2900.

All photos courtesy of AP Images—AP/Wide World Photos, Inc. except the following:
Topps, Inc. (7, 14, 20, 21, 26, 30, 34 both, 37, 40 both, 41 all, 43);
Andrew D. Bernstein/NBAE/Getty Images (27); Author's Collection (35 top left).
Special thanks to Topps, Inc.

Editor: Mike Kennedy
Associate Editor: Brian Fitzgerald
Designer: Ron Jaffe
Project Management: Black Book Partners, LLC.
Special thanks to Andy Buchanan, David Kennedy, Javier Perez, and Pam and Richard Donath.

Library of Congress Cataloging-in-Publication Data

Stewart, Mark, 1960-
  The Chicago Bulls / by Mark Stewart ; content consultant, Matt
Zeysing.
      p. cm.
  Summary: "Presents the history, accomplishments and key person-
alities of the Chicago Bulls basketball team. Includes timelines,
quotes, maps, glossary and websites"--Provided by publisher.
  Includes bibliographical references and index.
  ISBN-13: 978-1-59953-129-8 (library edition : alk. paper)
  ISBN-10: 1-59953-129-1 (library edition : alk. paper)
  1. Chicago Bulls (Basketball team)--History--Juvenile literature. I.
Title.
GV885.52.C45S74 2008
796.323'640977311--dc22
                                                    2007011706

Manufactured in the United States of America.

COVER PHOTO: Ben Gordon and Andres Nocioni celebrate a victory in 2007 with a mid-air bump.

Table of Contents

CHAPTER	PAGE
Meet the Bulls	4
Way Back When	6
The Team Today	10
Home Court	12
Dressed for Success	14
We Won!	16
Go-To Guys	20
On the Sidelines	24
One Great Day	26
Legend Has It	28
It Really Happened	30
Team Spirit	32
Timeline	34
Fun Facts	36
Talking Hoops	38
For the Record	40
Pinpoints	42
Play Ball	44
Glossary	46
Places to Go	47
Index	48

SPORTS WORDS & VOCABULARY WORDS: In this book, you will find many words that are new to you. You may also see familiar words used in new ways. The glossary on page 46 gives the meanings of basketball words, as well as "everyday" words that have special basketball meanings. These words appear in **bold type** throughout the book. The glossary on page 47 gives the meanings of vocabulary words that are not related to basketball. They appear in ***bold italic type*** throughout the book.

BASKETBALL SEASONS: Because each basketball season begins late in one year and ends early in the next, seasons are not named after years. Instead; they are written out as two years separated by a dash, for example 1944–45 or 2005–06.

Meet the Bulls

There are few things scarier than finding yourself in the path of an angry bull. During the 1990s, that is how most teams in the **National Basketball Association (NBA)** felt. The Chicago Bulls had the best player, most creative coach, and loudest fans. It was a lot of fun to root for the Bulls, and no fun to play against them.

The Bulls were successful because they made the most of all of their strengths. They shared the basketball on offense and learned how to help one another on defense. They liked how it felt to walk off the court a winner. All these years later, they have not lost that feeling.

This book tells the story of the Bulls. They play the game with great skill and a lot of heart. Their recipe for success is blending the talents and personalities of many different players. The Bulls always win as a team, no matter how brightly any of their stars shine.

Andres Nocioni and Ben Gordon exchange high fives. The Bulls look for players who know how to blend their different playing styles and skills in winning ways.

Way Back When

Chicago, Illinois has been an important center of **professional** basketball since the 1930s. Chicago Stadium was the site of the **World Professional Basketball Tournament** for 10 years beginning in 1939. The city was also home to several pro teams, including the Stags and the Zephyrs, who eventually became the Washington Wizards.

Despite Chicago's rich basketball history, the city did not have a successful NBA team until 1966, when the league decided to expand from nine teams to ten. Chicago was awarded the new club, which became known as the Bulls. They won 33 games in their first year—enough to make the **playoffs**. The team's leaders were guards Guy Rodgers and Jerry Sloan and forward Bob Boozer.

During the 1970s, the Bulls continued to improve. Their best player was Bob Love, a forward who could score, rebound, and play tough defense. The Bulls also had one of the NBA's top one-on-one players, forward Chet Walker. Super-competitive point guard Norm Van Lier led the club from the backcourt. Teammates and fans called him "Stormin' Norman" because of his *intense* desire to win. Chicago's defense was helped by its big centers, including Tom Boerwinkle, Clifford Ray, and Nate Thurmond. The Bulls came within one victory of reaching the **NBA Finals** in 1975.

NORM VAN LIER · G

The Bulls added stars such as Artis Gilmore, Reggie Theus, and Orlando Woolridge in the years that followed, but the team struggled to win. Their luck began to change in 1984, when they used the third pick in the **NBA draft** to select Michael Jordan. He was named the league's **Rookie of the Year** in 1985.

LEFT: Jerry Sloan drives to the hoop against the Milwaukee Bucks.
ABOVE: Norm Van Lier

There seemed to be no limit to Jordan's talent. He was the league's top scorer seven years in a row. Jordan was such an amazing player that his teammates often faded into the background. This prevented the Bulls from reaching the NBA Finals during the 1980s. More balanced, team-oriented opponents always defeated them in the playoffs.

The Bulls finally became a great team during the 1990s when they found the right players to surround Jordan. Scottie Pippen was a wonderful **all-around** forward who worked hard on offense and defense. He was joined by very strong **role players**, including Bill Cartwright, Horace Grant, Luc Longley, Toni Kukoc, Dennis Rodman, B.J. Armstrong, John Paxson, Steve Kerr, and Ron Harper.

The Bulls also made a great move by hiring Phil Jackson to coach the team. He taught the players to share the ball on offense, which created opportunities to score. Chicago's unselfish style of play helped the team win six NBA Championships.

The Bulls might have won even more had Jordan not left the game for most of two seasons. He returned to win three more scoring championships and two more **Most Valuable Player (MVP)** awards. In all, he was named the league's top player five times.

LEFT: Michael Jordan glides to the basket for a dunk. He was the greatest player in team history.   **ABOVE**: Scottie Pippen cuts to the hoop. He was the perfect player to pair with Jordan.

The Team Today

The Bulls may never have another player with the ability of Michael Jordan. They certainly cannot count on it. After Jordan left Chicago in 1998, the team began rebuilding with young players. It took the Bulls a few years to find a group with the right **team chemistry**. Once they did, the Bulls began winning again.

The Bulls are known for making smart trades and daring draft picks. They also have been willing to look overseas for players that can help them win. The team was successful with this *strategy* in the 1990s. The Bulls believe it will work again. By building a team around smart, talented players such as Kirk Hinrich, Luol Deng, and Ben Gordon, the Bulls created a solid foundation for the future.

Chicago fans hope to see another extraordinary player like Jordan some day. In the meantime, they take great pride in the Bulls whenever the team wins. They know that a victory in the NBA requires hard work and unselfish play—the same as it did when "MJ" wore the red, white, and black.

Kirk Hinrich and Luol Deng, two of the Bulls' young leaders. In 2006–07, they helped the team win its first playoff series since 1998.

Home Court

For more than 25 years, the Bulls called Chicago Stadium "home." This beautiful building was nicknamed the "Madhouse on Madison" because of how noisy it was when Chicago fans got excited. For a long time, it was the largest indoor arena in the world. Part of the basketball court from Chicago Stadium is now the floor of the trophy room in Michael Jordan's home.

The Bulls moved into the United Center at the start of the 1994–95 season. Jerry Reinsdorf, the Bulls' owner, teamed up with William Wirtz, the owner of the Chicago Blackhawks hockey team, to help build the arena. A statue of Jordan greets fans at the United Center's east side.

BY THE NUMBERS

- *There are 21,711 seats for basketball in the Bulls' arena.*
- *More than 20 million people have attended events in the Bulls' arena since it opened.*
- *As of 2007, the Bulls had retired four jersey numbers—4 (Jerry Sloan), 10 (Bob Love), 23 (Michael Jordan), and 33 (Scottie Pippen). The team has also honored coach Phil Jackson and Jerry Krause, who helped build the Bulls into a championship club.*

Fans get a good look at the action in the Bulls' arena.

Dressed for Success

The Bulls were named in honor of the Chicago Stockyards, where much of America's beef once came from. The team's founder, Dick Klein, asked for a *logo* that showed an angry bull or, as he put it, "a bull in a fight." The result was a red and black bull with red eyes and blood on the tips of his horns. Chicago's logo has changed little since then.

The team's uniform has always used red, white, and black. In the late 1960s, they featured warm-ups that also included the color pink. During the 1990s, the Bulls wore *pinstriped* uniforms. They also started wearing black shoes during the playoffs. This has since become a team *tradition*.

Chicago's most famous uniform may be the one that Michael Jordan wore after he came back from a brief retirement. The Bulls had retired his number 23, so he chose number 45 instead. When he changed back to 23 during the 1995 playoffs, the NBA fined the Bulls for switching the number without the league's approval. Jordan wore 23 from 1995–96 on.

Bob Love poses in the team's old warm-ups.

14

UNIFORM BASICS

The basketball uniform is very simple. It consists of a roomy top and baggy shorts.

- The top hangs from the shoulders, with big "scoops" for the arms and neck. This style has not changed much over the years.

- Shorts, however, have changed a lot. They used to be very short, so players could move their legs freely. In the last 20 years, shorts have gotten longer and much baggier.

Basketball uniforms look the same as they did long ago ... until you look very closely. In the old days, the shorts had belts and buckles. The tops were made of a thick cotton called "jersey," which got very heavy when players sweated. Later, uniforms were made of shiny **satin**. They may have looked great, but they did not "breathe." As a result, players got very hot! Today, most uniforms are made of **synthetic** materials that soak up sweat and keep the body cool.

Ben Wallace wears the Bulls' home uniform in a 2007 game. The team's logo can be seen on the side of his shorts.

We Won!

Michael Jordan had won every honor there was in the 1980s—except an NBA Championship. Two years in a row, the Bulls reached the **Eastern Conference Finals**, only to lose to the Detroit Pistons. In 1989–90, Phil Jackson became the team's coach. He knew the key to winning a title was convincing Jordan to use his talents to make the players around him better.

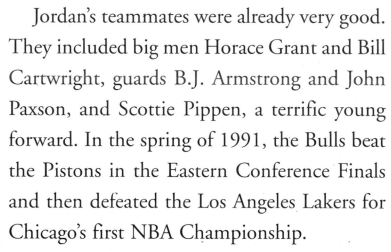

Jordan's teammates were already very good. They included big men Horace Grant and Bill Cartwright, guards B.J. Armstrong and John Paxson, and Scottie Pippen, a terrific young forward. In the spring of 1991, the Bulls beat the Pistons in the Eastern Conference Finals and then defeated the Los Angeles Lakers for Chicago's first NBA Championship.

One year later, the Bulls played the Portland Trail Blazers for the title. Jordan, the NBA's best player, was guarded by Clyde Drexler, its second-best player. Drexler simply could not stop him. After Chicago's six-game victory, he said, "Going into the series, I thought Michael had two thousand moves. I was wrong—he has three thousand!"

The 1993 NBA Finals brought Jordan and the Bulls face-to-face with Charles Barkley and the Phoenix Suns. The two stars fought hard, and after five games the Bulls were ahead three games to two. The Suns would not give up. They led the sixth game 98–96 with just a few seconds to go. Chicago fans were worried their third championship might be slipping away.

Jordan got the ball but was too well defended. He passed to Pippen, who did not have a shot either. Pippen passed to Grant. Even though Grant was close to the basket, he saw Paxson standing alone beyond the **3-point line** and whipped the ball to him. Paxson took a long shot that swished through the net to give the Bulls their championship "three-peat."

LEFT: Horace Grant dunks against the Pistons.   **ABOVE**: Michael Jordan celebrates after winning the 1993 NBA Championship.

The Bulls returned to the NBA Finals three years later after *steamrolling* through the regular season with a record of 72–10. Jordan and Pippen were still the club's stars. Their new teammates included Dennis Rodman, Toni Kukoc, Ron Harper, Luc Longley, and Steve Kerr. They easily defeated the Seattle Supersonics for their fourth championship.

In the 1997 NBA Finals, the Bulls battled the Utah Jazz. Again, just one win from the title, Chicago faced a tense situation in Game 6. With time ticking away late in the fourth quarter, the score was tied 86–86. Everyone in Chicago Stadium knew Jordan would get the ball. He faked out three Utah players and then suddenly fired a pass to Kerr, who had been ice-cold during the series. Kerr calmly swished a 20-foot shot for the victory.

History repeated one year and one day later, as Jordan again helped beat the Jazz in Game 6 of the NBA Finals. This time, he made the winning shot himself. With the Bulls behind 86–85 and less than 10 seconds on the clock, Jordan drove to the basket, then quickly stopped and rose for a jump shot. As the ball went through the basket, Jordan punched the air in a joyous victory celebration. It was the last shot he would ever take for the Bulls, who had their sixth NBA Championship in eight remarkable seasons.

LEFT: Steve Kerr launches the winning shot against the Jazz in 1997.
ABOVE: Michael Jordan releases the final shot of his great career with the Bulls. This basket won the 1998 NBA Finals for Chicago.

19

Go-To Guys

To be a true star in the NBA, you need more than a great shot. You have to be a "go-to guy"—someone teammates trust to make the winning play when the seconds are ticking away in a big game. Bulls fans have had a lot to cheer about over the years, including these great stars …

THE PIONEERS

JERRY SLOAN   GUARD

JERRY SLOAN   6' 5" Guard

- BORN: 3/28/1942
- PLAYED FOR TEAM: 1966–67 TO 1975–76

Jerry Sloan never thought of himself as a star, so he played every game as if the team might cut him that day. That helped him become the best defensive guard in the NBA. Sloan was not afraid to challenge bigger players for baskets and rebounds.

BOB LOVE   6' 8" Forward

- BORN: 12/8/1942   • PLAYED FOR TEAM: 1968–69 TO 1976–77

Players who matched up against Bob Love never got a rest. He could score from anywhere on the court and was one of the best defensive players in the league. Love averaged more than 25 points a game twice and made the NBA **All-Defensive Team** three times.

ABOVE: Jerry Sloan   **RIGHT**: Chet Walker

CHET WALKER   6' 7" Forward

- BORN: 2/22/1940
- PLAYED FOR TEAM: 1969–70 TO 1974–75

Chet Walker was nicknamed the "Jet" because of his speed and leaping ability. On a team known mainly for its strong defense, he provided important points at "crunch time." Walker loved pressure and was one of the best free-throw shooters in team history.

NORM VAN LIER   6' 2" Guard

- BORN: 4/1/1947
- PLAYED FOR TEAM: 1971–72 TO 1977–78

The Bulls drafted Norm Van Lier in 1969, quickly traded him, and then spent more than two years trying to get him back. He was a *tenacious* defensive player and an unselfish passer. For many years, Van Lier held the NBA record for the longest basket—an amazing 84 feet.

ARTIS GILMORE   7' 2" Center

- BORN: 9/21/1948
- PLAYED FOR TEAM: 1976–77 TO 1981–82 & 1987–88

Towering Artis Gilmore came to the Bulls after the **American Basketball Association (ABA)** went out of business in 1976. Few players in the NBA could match Gilmore's strength. He was an **All-Star** four times with the Bulls.

MICHAEL JORDAN 6' 6" Guard

- BORN: 2/17/1963
- PLAYED FOR TEAM: 1984–85 TO 1992–93 & 1994–95 TO 1997–98

Michael Jordan was already an excellent all-around player when he joined the Bulls, and he kept getting better and better. He led Chicago to six championships and was named MVP of the NBA Finals each time. No basketball player has ever captured the world's imagination as Jordan did.

SCOTTIE PIPPEN 6' 7" Guard/Forward

- BORN: 9/25/1965
- PLAYED FOR TEAM: 1987–88 TO 1997–98 & 2003-04

Scottie Pippen had the talent to play every position on the court, and sometimes he did. His ability to guard an opponent's best player was a key to the Bulls' six championships. Pippen was voted to the NBA's All-Defensive Team 10 times.

HORACE GRANT 6' 10" Forward

- BORN: 7/4/1965   • PLAYED FOR TEAM: 1987–88 TO 1993–94

Horace Grant was one of the best defensive players and rebounders in the NBA. If teams paid too much attention to Jordan and Pippen, Grant **chipped in** with baskets from the outside. His identical twin, Harvey, was also an NBA player.

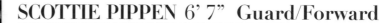

ABOVE: Scottie Pippen and Michael Jordan celebrate their 1997 championship. **TOP RIGHT**: Kirk Hinrich   **BOTTOM RIGHT**: Ben Gordon

KIRK HINRICH   6' 3" Guard

• BORN: 1/2/1981   • FIRST SEASON WITH TEAM: 2003–04

Kirk Hinrich wanted to play for the Bulls from the time he was a kid. His hustle and knowledge of the game reminded old-time Chicago fans of Jerry Sloan. His desire to win gave them great hope for the team's future.

LUOL DENG   6' 9" Forward

• BORN: 4/16/1985   • FIRST SEASON WITH TEAM: 2004–05

Luol Deng played just one season in college before coming to the Bulls as a teenager. He needed only a few games before he looked like an old pro. A member of Sudan's Dinka tribe, Deng learned basketball from Manute Bol, another Dinka tribesman who starred in the NBA for many years.

BEN GORDON   6' 3" Guard

• BORN: 4/4/1983   • FIRST SEASON WITH TEAM: 2004–05

The Bulls surprised many experts when they selected Ben Gordon with the third pick in the 2004 NBA draft. Gordon knew the team had not made a mistake. He quickly became one of the league's best **fourth-quarter players**.

23

On the Sidelines

The Bulls have had some of the NBA's most successful and *innovative* coaches. Their first coach was Johnny Kerr, who later became the team's play-by-play announcer. He led the Bulls to the playoffs in their first year. Kerr was followed by Dick Motta. Under Motta, Chicago became an excellent defensive team.

During the 1980s, the Bulls were coached by Jerry Sloan, Paul Westhead, Kevin Loughery, Stan Albeck, and Doug Collins. All were respected NBA leaders, but none could find the key to winning a championship.

In 1989, Jerry Krause, Chicago's boss off the court, made an important decision. He chose Phil Jackson to coach the Bulls. Jackson and assistant coach Tex Winter designed plays that used all of the club's talent, not just Michael Jordan's. They called their system the "Triangle Offense." It helped the Bulls win six championships.

Phil Jackson hugs Michael Jordan after Chicago's fourth NBA Championship. Jackson led the Bulls to six titles in all.

One Great Day

When Michael Jordan joined the Chicago Bulls in 1984, he thought of himself as a winner. He had just led the **U.S. Olympic team** to a gold medal. Two years earlier, he had guided his college team to the **National Championship**. Naturally, he assumed that winning an NBA Championship would be the next step.

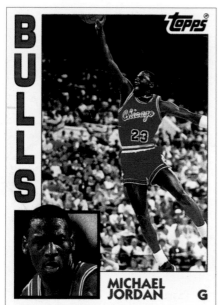

Over the next six seasons, Jordan and the Bulls fell short each year. It seems incredible now, but back then many thought that Jordan was too selfish as a player to win an NBA Championship. This criticism *motivated* him to try even harder for a title.

In 1991, after years of disappointment, the Bulls reached the NBA Finals. Jordan and his teammates faced the Los Angeles Lakers. Thanks to Chicago coach Phil Jackson, Jordan now understood that the key to winning was getting the entire team to play together. He did just that.

No one was more surprised than the Lakers. When the series started, they were only worried about Jordan. But Los Angeles quickly learned that the Bulls were a complete team. Chicago won three of the first four games against the Lakers. By Game 5, Los Angeles had no idea how to beat the Bulls. Chicago won 108–101 and claimed the first championship in team history.

Almost everyone on the Bulls contributed to the victory. Scottie Pippen led the team with 32 points and 13 rebounds. Bill Cartwright, Chicago's center, had seven **assists**. John Paxson made five baskets in the last four minutes and finished with 20 points. And Jordan? All he did was score 30 points with 10 assists and five steals. An hour after the game ended, he still had tears in his eyes.

"I never thought I'd be this emotional," Jordan said. "I always had faith I'd get this ring one day."

LEFT: Michael Jordan was nicknamed "Air Jordan"—this trading card shows why.　**ABOVE**: Jordan is the man in the middle of Chicago's 1991 title celebration.

Legend Has It

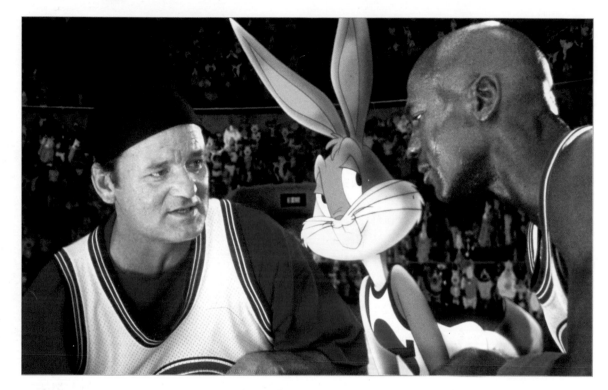

Which Bull once dunked on a space alien?

LEGEND HAS IT that Michael Jordan did. In 1996, he starred in a movie called *Space Jam*. In the story, Jordan agrees to help Bugs Bunny and his friends win their freedom from an evil slave trader and his space-alien superstars in a basketball game. The contest ends on a spectacular dunk by Jordan.

ABOVE: Actor Bill Murray, Bugs Bunny, and Michael Jordan make a plan to beat the aliens in a scene from *Space Jam*.   **RIGHT**: Kirk Hinrich

Was it "destiny" that made Kirk Hinrich a Chicago Bull?

LEGEND HAS IT that it was. When Hinrich was a seventh grader, the students in his class were asked to write down what they thought they would be doing in 10 years. Their answers were then sealed in envelopes. In 2005, Hinrich's mom opened the envelope and read his prediction—"I'm going to be a starting point guard for the Chicago Bulls."

Who was the Bulls' greatest 3-point shooter?

LEGEND HAS IT that Craig Hodges was. A valuable **substitute** on the Chicago teams of the early 1990s, he would come off the bench and give the Bulls instant offense. Hodges also won the 3-Point Shootout at the NBA All-Star Game three times. In one of those shootouts, he made 19 shots in a row. In recent years, Ben Gordon has come closest to "challenging" Hodges as Chicago's best long-distance man. He once tried nine 3-pointers in a game against the Washington Wizards and hit every one of them!

It Really Happened

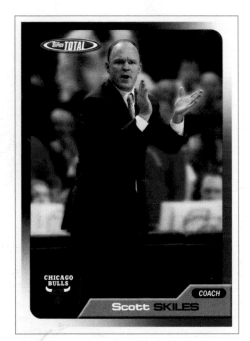

No one likes to sit on the bench during a basketball game, especially NBA players. However, a winning team depends on more than its starting five. During the 2006–07 season, the Bulls had enough talent to make Ben Gordon their sixth man. Chicago coach Scott Skiles wanted to save his hot-shooting guard for just the right moments. The fourth quarter soon became "Gordon Time."

On December 27th, Gordon watched the opening tip-off against the Miami Heat from the sidelines. Skiles sent him into the game soon enough, and by the end of the third quarter Gordon had 21 points. He was just getting started. In the fourth quarter, Gordon kept shooting and kept making his shots. He scored 19 more points to finish with 40. The Bulls needed every one of them to hold off a furious comeback by Miami. They won 109–103.

ABOVE: This 2006 trading card shows Scott Skiles cheering for his Bulls.
RIGHT: Ben Gordon scores against the Miami Heat.

Six days later, Gordon was sitting on the bench again when a game between the Bulls and Phoenix Suns began. It was another close, exciting contest. Gordon scored 24 points in the first three quarters, then added 17 in the final period to finish with 41. Gordon's best was not good enough, however. Chicago lost 97–96.

By that time, Gordon liked his role as Chicago's "super-sub." He also learned he had set a record. Gordon was the first player in the history of the NBA to come off the bench and score 40 points twice in the same week.

Team Spirit

Basketball fans have had much to cheer about since the Bulls came to Chicago in the 1960s. Over the years, they have seen what it takes to win an NBA Championship—good defense and strong rebounding. Today, Bulls fans applaud just as hard when a player dives for a loose ball as they do for a successful 3-point shot.

A Bulls game looks a lot different today than it did when the team began. Benny the Bull, a big red mascot, roams the stands and sidelines. He also performs dunking exhibitions and dirt-bike stunts. The Luvabulls dance team takes the floor during breaks in the action to entertain the crowd.

The loudest cheers at Bulls games are often saved for the Matadors, one of the strangest cheerleading squads in all of sports. The Matadors are made up of Chicago's "biggest" basketball fans. This group of large men thunders onto the court during timeouts and dances for about a minute. The Matadors bring smiles—and looks of wonder—to thousands of faces at every Bulls game.

Benny the Bull is one of the NBA's most popular mascots.

Timeline

The basketball season is played from October through June. That means each season takes place at the end of one year and halfway through the next. In this timeline, the accomplishments of the Bulls are shown by season.

1968–69
Jerry Sloan is voted to the All-Defensive Team.

1985–86
Michael Jordan scores 63 points in a playoff game against the Boston Celtics.

1966–67
The Bulls win 33 games in their first season.

1970–71
Chet Walker is the NBA's best free-throw shooter.

1981–82
Artis Gilmore leads the league in **field goal percentage**.

CHICAGO

CHET WALKER
BULLS' FORWARD

Chet Walker

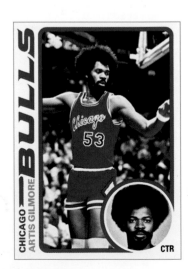

BULLS

CHICAGO ARTIS GILMORE

CTR

Artis Gilmore

The Bulls "three-peat" pennant from 1993.

Ben Gordon, a star for the 2006–07 team.

1992–93
The Bulls complete their first championship "three-peat."

1995–96
The Bulls set an NBA record with 72 wins.

2006–07
The Bulls win their first playoff series since the Michael Jordan *era*.

1990–91
The Bulls win their first NBA Championship.

1993–94
Scottie Pippen is named All-Star Game MVP.

1997–98
The Bulls win their sixth NBA Championship.

Phil Jackson accepts the award as the NBA's best coach in 1996.

Fun Facts

PASSING INTEREST

The Bulls have been a good passing team since their very first season. Guy Rodgers started the tradition. He led the NBA in assists in 1966–67 and had 24 in one game against the New York Knicks that year.

CHAIRMEN OF THE BOARDS

Two Bulls have led the league in rebounding—Dennis Rodman and Charles Oakley. Rodman did it three seasons in a row starting in 1995–96. Chicago won the NBA Championship each year.

KICKING IT

Luol Deng entered the NBA with very good footwork for a player his size. He said it came from playing soccer as a teenager. He was invited to join England's Under–15 soccer squad but chose basketball instead.

ABOVE: Dennis Rodman grabs a rebound.
RIGHT: Bob Love

GONE BATTY

In the middle of his career, Michael Jordan shocked the world by announcing he was quitting basketball to try baseball. He played one season in the minor leagues for the Chicago White Sox. Jordan then returned to the Bulls and won three more NBA Championships.

LOVE CONQUERS ALL

After his NBA career was over, Bob Love struggled to find a good job because of his severe *stutter*. He conquered the problem with years of speech therapy. Love later became Director of Community Affairs for the Bulls and a popular motivational speaker.

BOB LOVE   FORWARD

FOREIGN AID

The 2006-07 Bulls had six players born outside the United States—Martynas Andriuskevicius (Lithuania), Luol Deng (Sudan), Ben Gordon (England), Viktor Khryapa (Ukraine), Andres Nocioni (Argentina), and Thabo Sefolosha (Switzerland).

Talking Hoops

"The more intensely you can get into the game, the better you are going to play."
—*Toni Kukoc, on what it takes to be a good player off the bench*

"I never practice the fancy stuff. If I thought about a move, I'd probably turn the ball over. I just look at a situation in the air, adjust, create, and let instincts take over."
—*Michael Jordan, on his most amazing shots*

"Sometimes a player's greatest challenge is **coming to grips** with his role on the team."
—*Scottie Pippen, on being the Bulls' "number-two" star behind Jordan*

"Saving a basket is just as good as making one."
—*Jerry Sloan, on the importance of playing defense*

"It's not like I'm out there talking noise and getting in people's faces, but I am confident. That's what makes great players. I can't think of one great player that doesn't show confidence."

—*Kirk Hinrich, on playing with pride*

"Love is the force that ignites the spirit and binds teams together."

—*Phil Jackson, on what makes a championship team*

"If you reach the top of the mountain, then there's no place else to go. So you set your sights on the highest mountain and hope someday you'll reach it."

—*Artis Gilmore, on setting your goals high*

"The game hasn't become any easier, but I've become more experienced and that's a big thing in this league."

—*Ben Gordon, on what it means to be an NBA veteran*

LEFT: Toni Kukoc   **ABOVE**: Phil Jackson

For the Record

The great Bulls teams and players have left their marks on the record books. These are the "best of the best" …

Scottie Pippen

Elton Brand

BULLS AWARD WINNERS

WINNER	AWARD	SEASON
Johnny Kerr	NBA Coach of the Year	1966–67
Dick Motta	NBA Coach of the Year	1970–71
Michael Jordan	NBA Rookie of the Year	1984–85
Michael Jordan	NBA Slam Dunk Champion	1986–87
Michael Jordan	NBA Slam Dunk Champion	1987–88
Michael Jordan	NBA All-Star Game MVP	1987–88
Michael Jordan	NBA Defensive Player of the Year	1987–88
Michael Jordan	NBA Most Valuable Player	1987–88
Craig Hodges	NBA 3-Point Shootout Champion	1989–90
Craig Hodges	NBA 3-Point Shootout Champion	1990–91
Michael Jordan	NBA Most Valuable Player	1990–91
Michael Jordan	NBA Finals MVP	1990–91
Craig Hodges	NBA 3-Point Shootout Champion	1991–92
Michael Jordan	NBA Most Valuable Player	1991–92
Michael Jordan	NBA Finals MVP	1991–92
Michael Jordan	NBA Finals MVP	1992–93
Scottie Pippen	NBA All-Star Game MVP	1993–94
Michael Jordan	NBA All-Star Game MVP	1995–96
Phil Jackson	NBA Coach of the Year	1995–96
Toni Kukoc	NBA Sixth Man Award	1995–96
Michael Jordan	NBA Most Valuable Player	1995–96
Michael Jordan	NBA Finals MVP	1995–96
Steve Kerr	NBA 3-Point Shootout Champion	1996–97
Michael Jordan	NBA Finals MVP	1996–97
Michael Jordan	NBA Most Valuable Player	1997–98
Michael Jordan	NBA Finals MVP	1997–98
Elton Brand	NBA co-Rookie of the Year	1999–00
Ben Gordon	NBA Sixth Man Award	2004–05

BULLS ACHIEVEMENTS

ACHIEVEMENT	SEASON
Midwest Division Champions	1974–75
Central Division Champions	1990–91
Eastern Conference Champions	1990–91
NBA Champions	1990–91
Central Division Champions	1991–92
Eastern Conference Champions	1991–92
NBA Champions	1991–92
Central Division Champions	1992–93
Eastern Conference Champions	1992–93
NBA Champions	1992–93
Central Division Champions	1995–96
Eastern Conference Champions	1995–96
NBA Champions	1995–96
Central Division Champions	1996–97
Eastern Conference Champions	1996–97
NBA Champions	1996–97
Central Division Champions	1997–98
Eastern Conference Champions	1997–98
NBA Champions	1997–98

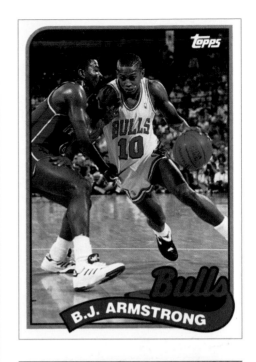

ABOVE: The stars of the 1974–75 Bulls.
RIGHT: B.J. Armstrong and Horace Grant, important members
of the championship teams of the early 1990s.

Pinpoints

The history of a basketball team is made up of many smaller stories. These stories take place all over the map—not just in the city a team calls "home." Match the pushpins on these maps to the Team Facts and you will begin to see the story of the Bulls unfold!

TEAM FACTS

1   Chicago, Illinois—*The Bulls have played here since 1966.*

2   Sioux City, Iowa—*Kirk Hinrich was born here.*

3   Benton Harbor, Michigan—*Chet Walker was born here.*

4   East Liverpool, Ohio—*Norm Van Lier was born here.*

5   Brooklyn, New York—*Michael Jordan was born here.*

6   Hamburg, Arkansas—*Scottie Pippen was born here.*

7   Bastrop, Louisiana—*Bob Love was born here.*

8   Los Angeles, California—*The Bulls won their first NBA Championship here.*

9   London, England—*Ben Gordon was born here.*

10   Split, Croatia—*Toni Kukoc was born here.*

11   Wau, Sudan—*Luol Deng was born here.*

12   Santa Fe, Argentina—*Andres Nocioni was born here.*

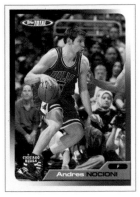

Andres Nocioni

Play Ball

Basketball is a sport played by two teams of five players. NBA games have four 12-minute quarters—48 minutes in all—and the team that scores the most points when time has run out is the winner. Most baskets count for two points. Players who make shots from beyond the 3-point line receive an extra point. Baskets made from the free-throw line count for one point. Free throws are penalty shots awarded to a team, usually after an opponent has committed a foul. A foul is called when one player makes hard contact with another.

Players can move around all they want, but the player with the ball cannot. He must bounce the ball with one hand or the other (but never both) in order to go from one part of the court to another. As long as he keeps "dribbling," he can keep moving.

In the NBA, teams must attempt a shot within 24 seconds, so there is little time to waste. The job of the defense is to make it as difficult as possible for the offense to take a good shot—and to grab the ball if the other team shoots and misses.

This may sound simple, but anyone who has played the game knows that basketball can be very complicated. Every player on the court has a job to do. Different players have different strengths and weaknesses. The coach must mix these players in just the right way and teach them to work together as one.

The more you play and watch basketball, the more "little things" you are likely to notice. The next time you watch a game, look for these plays:

PLAY LIST

ALLEY-OOP—A play in which the passer throws the ball just to the side of the rim—so a teammate can catch it and dunk in one motion.

BACK-DOOR PLAY—A play in which the passer waits for a teammate to fake the defender away from the basket—then throws him the ball when he cuts back toward the basket.

KICK-OUT—A play in which the ball handler waits for the defense to surround him—then quickly passes to a teammate who is open for an outside shot. The ball is not really kicked in this play; the term comes from the action of pinball machines.

NO-LOOK PASS—A play in which a passer fools the defense by looking in one direction, then making a surprise pass to a teammate in another direction.

PICK-AND-ROLL—A play in which one player blocks, or "picks off," a teammate's defender with his body, then in the confusion cuts to the basket for a pass.

Glossary

BASKETBALL WORDS TO KNOW

3-POINT LINE—The line on the court that separates 2-point baskets from 3-point baskets. A shot made from behind this line is worth three points.

ALL-AROUND—Good at all parts of the game.

ALL-DEFENSIVE TEAM—An honor given at the end of each season to the NBA's best defensive players at each position.

ALL-STAR—A player selected to play in the annual All-Star Game.

AMERICAN BASKETBALL ASSOCIATION (ABA)—The basketball league that played for nine seasons starting in 1967. Prior to the 1976–77 season, four ABA teams joined the NBA, and the rest went out of business.

ASSISTS—Passes that lead to successful shots.

EASTERN CONFERENCE FINALS—The playoff series that determines which team from the East will play the best team from the West for the NBA Championship.

FIELD GOAL PERCENTAGE—A statistic that measures shooting accuracy.

FOURTH-QUARTER PLAYERS—Players who are at their best in the final 12 minutes of a game.

MOST VALUABLE PLAYER (MVP)—The award given each year to the league's best player; also given to the best player in the league finals and All-Star Game.

NATIONAL BASKETBALL ASSOCIATION (NBA)—The professional league that has been operating since 1946–47.

NATIONAL CHAMPIONSHIP—The title that college basketball teams play for at the end of each season.

NBA DRAFT—The annual meeting where teams pick from a group of the best college players.

NBA FINALS—The playoff series that decides the champion of the league.

PLAYOFFS—The games played after the season to determine the league champion.

PROFESSIONAL—Describes a player or team that plays a sport for money. College players are not paid, so they are considered "amateurs."

ROLE PLAYERS—People who are asked to do specific things when they are in a game.

ROOKIE OF THE YEAR—The annual award given to the league's best first-year player.

SUBSTITUTE—A player who begins most games on the bench.

TEAM CHEMISTRY—The ability of teammates to work together well. Winning teams often have good team chemistry.

U.S. OLYMPIC TEAM—A group of players that represents the United States in the Olympics, an international sports competition held every four years.

WORLD PROFESSIONAL BASKETBALL TOURNAMENT—The tournament for professional basketball teams held every year from 1939 to 1948.

OTHER WORDS TO KNOW

CHIPPED IN—Contributed in a small but important way.

COMING TO GRIPS—Grasping an idea.

ERA—A period of time in history.

INNOVATIVE—Able to come up with new ideas.

INTENSE—Very strong or very deep.

LOGO—A symbol or design that represents a company or team.

MOTIVATED—Inspired to achieve.

PINSTRIPED—Designed with thin stripes.

SATIN—A smooth, shiny fabric.

STEAMROLLING—Flattening everything in its path.

STRATEGY—A plan or method for succeeding.

STUTTER—A speech disorder.

SYNTHETIC—Made in a laboratory, not in nature.

TENACIOUS—Never giving up.

TRADITION—A belief or custom that is passed down from generation to generation.

Places to Go

ON THE ROAD

CHICAGO BULLS
1901 West Madison Street
Chicago, Illinois 60612
(312) 455-4000

NAISMITH MEMORIAL BASKETBALL HALL OF FAME
1000 West Columbus Avenue
Springfield, Massachusetts 01105
(877) 4HOOPLA

ON THE WEB

THE NATIONAL BASKETBALL ASSOCIATION   www.nba.com
- *Learn more about the league's teams, players, and history*

THE CHICAGO BULLS   www.bulls.com
- *Learn more about the Chicago Bulls*

THE BASKETBALL HALL OF FAME   www.hoophall.com
- *Learn more about history's greatest players*

ON THE BOOKSHELF

To learn more about the sport of basketball, look for these books at your library or bookstore:
- Thomas, Keltie. *How Basketball Works.* Berkeley, CA: Maple Tree Press, distributed through Publishers Group West, 2005.
- Hareas, John. *Basketball.* New York, NY: Dorling Kindersley, 2005.
- Hughes, Morgan. *Basketball.* Vero Beach, FL: Rourke Publishing, 2005.

Index

PAGE NUMBERS IN **BOLD** REFER TO ILLUSTRATIONS.

Albeck, Stan 25
Andriuskevicius, Martynas 37
Armstrong, B.J. 9, 16, **41**
Barkley, Charles 17
Benny the Bull.................**32**, 33
Boerwinkle, Tom........................7
Bol, Manute...............................23
Boozer, Bob 6
Brand, Elton **40**, **40**
Bugs Bunny.....................28, **28**
Cartwright, Bill 9, 16, 27
Chicago Stadium 6, 13, 18
Chicago Stags 6
Chicago Zephyrs 6
Collins, Doug 25
Deng, Luol **10**, 11,
        23, 36, 37, 43
Drexler, Clyde 16
Gilmore, Artis 7, 21, 34, **34**, 39
Gordon, Ben **4**, 11, **23,**
        23, 29, 30, 31,
        31, **35**, 37, 39, 43
Grant, Harvey 22
Grant, Horace 9, 16, **16**,
        17, 22, **41**
Harper, Ron 9, 18
Hinrich, Kirk...............**10**, 11, 23,
        23, 29, **29**, 39, 43
Hodges, Craig.....................29, 40
Jackson, Phil 9, 13,
        16, **24**, 25,
        26, **35**, 39, **39**, 40
Jordan, Michael 7, **8**, 9, 11,
        13, 14, 16, 17,
        17, 18, 19, **19**, 22,
        22, **24**, 25, 26, **26**, 27, **27**,
        28, **28**, 34, 35, 37, 38, 40, 43
Kerr, Johnny 25, 40

Kerr, Steve 9, 18, **18**, 19, 40
Khryapa, Viktor 37
Klein, Dick 14
Krause, Jerry 13, 25
Kukoc, Toni ..9, 18, 38, **38**, 40, 43
Longley, Luc 9, 18
Loughery, Kevin 25
Love, Bob 6, 13, **14**, 20,
        37, **37**, **41**, 43
Luvabulls 33
Matadors 33
Motta, Dick 25, 40
Murray, Bill **28**
Nocioni, Andres **4**, 37, 43, **43**
Oakley, Charles 36
Paxson, John 9, 16, 17, 27
Pippen, Scottie 9, **9**, 13, 16,
        17, 18, 22, **22**,
        27, 35, 38, 40, **40**, 43
Ray, Clifford 7
Reinsdorf, Jerry 13
Rodgers, Guy 6, 36
Rodman, Dennis 9, 18, 36, **36**
Sefolosha, Thabo 37
Skiles, Scott 30, **30**
Sloan, Jerry 6, **6**, 13, 20,
        20, 23, 25, 34, 38
Theus, Reggie 7
Thurmond, Nate 7, **41**
United Center **12**, 13
Van Lier, Norm 7, **7**, 21, **41**, 43
Walker, Chet 7, 21, **21**,
        34, **34**, **41**, 43
Wallace, Ben **15**
Westhead, Paul..........................25
Winter, Tex 25
Wirtz, William 13
Woolridge, Orlando 7

The Team

MARK STEWART has written more than 20 books on basketball, and over 100 sports books for kids. He grew up in New York City during the 1960s rooting for the Knicks and Nets, and now takes his two daughters, Mariah and Rachel, to watch them play. Mark comes from a family of writers. His grandfather was Sunday Editor of *The New York Times* and his mother was Articles Editor of *The Ladies' Home Journal* and *McCall's*. Mark has profiled hundreds of athletes over the last 20 years. He has also written several books about his native New York, and New Jersey, his home today. Mark is a graduate of Duke University, with a degree in History. He lives with his daughters and wife Sarah overlooking Sandy Hook, New Jersey.

MATT ZEYSING is the resident historian at the Basketball Hall of Fame in Springfield, Massachusetts. His research interests include the origins of the game of basketball, the development of professional basketball in the first half of the 20th century, and the culture and meaning of basketball in American society.